Journey

from pathways to poems

Sue Johnson

&

Bob Woodroofe

The Greenwood Press

First published in 2017
This impression 2019

Greenwood Press
38 Birch Avenue
Evesham
Worcs. WR11 1YJ

Tel 01386 446477

http://www.greenwoodpress.co.uk

Many of these poems have previously been published in various poetry magazines and performed at readings.

Cover photographs
Sue Johnson & Bob Woodroofe

© Copyright 2017 & 2019
Sue Johnson & Bob Woodroofe

Sue Johnson & Bob Woodroofe have asserted their rights under the Copyright, Design & Patents Act 1988 to be identified as the authors of this work.

A CIP catalogue record for this book is available from the British Library

ISBN 978-0-9521165-9-2

Introduction

from pathways to poems

The paths we have taken
The things we have seen
The words we have found
This is our Journey

Dedication

This collection is dedicated to both our mothers

Gone but not forgotten

Jean Bloss

11th September 1926 to 8th April 2011

&

Nancy Joan Woodroofe (Min)

17th August 1917 to 11th September 2008

Contents

1 Glastonbury
2 Cross of light
3 Starlings
4 Murmuration
5 Gannets
6 Fifteen seconds
7 Bredon Hill
8 Hearts and shadows
9 Other side
10 From the other side
11 Beach walk in rain
12 Portheras
13 Holy well - Madron
14 Saint.Juliot's
15 18 Folgate street
16 18 Folgate street
17 Whitstable
18 Crab and winkle way
19 Treasures
20 Whitstable
21 Straggle
22 Absent
23 Iona
24 Driven
25 Tiddesley wood
26 The wood of Tidi
27 Geological laboratory
28 By the wind sailor
29 Mrs Humphrey's House
30 The Selkie's song
31 Meditation
32 Farewell
33 Mayhill
34 Sometime after 5.17am
35 Royal Mail
36 Island of the bards
37 The fairy glen
38 Fairy glen
39 Journey
40 Journey
41 Evesham - riverbank
42 Rush hour
43 Blue Pig Gallery Lewis
44 Time and tide
45 Callanish
46 Calanais
47 Tyn y Cwm
48 Estuary
49 Dream
50 Miner
51 Before the workshop
52 Selbourne
53 Cragg Sisters Tea Room
54 Flint strand
55 The Boat House
56 The Worm

Glastonbury

A suited businessman
looks out of place
amid the chaos and clamour
of café and street
where the shops are named
'Bedlam', 'The Magpie's Nest'
and 'Cat & Cauldron.'

I sit in my favourite window seat
in the Mocha Berry Café
glad to be back here despite the dark clouds
and the old penny sized raindrops
hitting the pavement outside.
I feel the energy vibrate
through the soles of my boots,
healing my spirit,
giving it wings again.

Cross of Light

A small cross, just a cheap
trinket on a board. You hardly
glanced, but it caught
your eye. You look
again, smooth but
not perfect, tiny pits
and bubbles betray
a natural origin. Colour
glows in your palm,
A strange feeling,
soothing to caress, as if you receive something from it each
time you touch. Whatever is inside slowly radiates out,
light and warmth flows into your fingers. A pure water,
clean air, blue sky peace, from far away, from a
distant land. Carved from amber, fossilised pine
resin. Brought from abroad, once a year, on a
pilgrimage from
Russia. From Grishino,
far in the North, on the
banks of the river
Vashenka, from the
International Centre
of Light. That light
pours from the small
cross. So much in such
a tiny object gives
such pleasure, invokes
these thoughts. A talisman
of peace, of hope, for us all.

Starlings

A crowd gathers as the sun's fire fades
over pale reed beds.
A shimmering near full moon rises
We wait
and wait, eyes turned skywards.

It begins with a few at first
then they gather in numbers
swirl across the landscape
now fish shaped
now a spiral
fluid as iron filings or mercury.

Then as the sky turns pink
a black rain shower of them falls
ripples across the reed beds
like an incoming tide.
The clamour of their voices
is raging water over rocks.

The moon rises higher. They quieten.
Darkness falls.
People and dogs flow back to the car park.

Murmuration

The sunlit gold of reed against dark water.
A black cross of cormorant beats overhead
through clear sky adorned with pink clouds.
The first few flight in low over the trees.
Then with an audible hiss through the air
dark clouds materialise in sunset sky.
The whisper of thousands of pairs of wings
that coalesce and the ballet begins.

Wave after wave wheel and swoop together,
whirl and swirl, first one way and then the other.
Flocks thicken darker as they ball tighter,
then fan out again, let the light back through.
Suddenly heavy they fall from sky.
A black rain tumbles down into the dusk,
funnels ever denser into the reeds.
Ducks disturbed from rest erupt from below.

A stately Heron flaps upwards and away.
Confused Lapwings circle round and around.
The noise begins, the gossip of Starlings,
one to another, shared with their neighbours.
Building slowly up to a crescendo,
louder now, drowns everything else out.
The babble of sound continues until
it gradually fades as night descends.

Other sounds become audible, somewhere
the drone of a plane, the tolling of bells,
the murmured wonder of the watching crowd
as the heath descends into quiet calm.

Gannets

look down from the top
of green patterned cliffs
to where the sea boils like milk far below

the east wind buffets our faces
carries a hint of rain

find the white arch
where foam crashes in and out
and the smell of nesting places rises
with the tide of sound

watch as they soar on air currents
lemon heads focused on grey sea below
white bodies crucifixed
black wingtips pointed downwards

searching

Fifteen seconds

By day not a flicker,
cliff and beach reflect sun
from face and grain.
When night falls it comes alive,
circles, sweeps over rooftops.

From 85 feet, shot through
disordered molecules of sand.
Brittle discs surrounded
by thinning concentric rings.
Refracting prisms revolve
produce parallel beams,
four short pulses, a pause,
fifteen seconds in all.
Again and again,
on and on till morn.

They work to the ingrained rhythm,
first light, then dark,
then light once more.
Deliver milk, post letters,
impale rag and lug on shore.
Caught in the glare,
migrants skulk in scrub,
gannets white against cliff white,
a badger blinks and pauses
atop the Dane's dyke.

The original still stands
but now the new tower
supports Fresnel lenses
through which 1000 watts
light the head of Flamborough.

Bredon Hill

I climb to where harebells dance
in late August sun
knowing you will never dance
on this earth again.

I feel sick with longing for you
but know the only way is forward
with my life.

As I look at the names
written in stones by the old fort
I feel an urge to create
a memorial for you.

I remember how Mum said
your beliefs were almost Celtic
a grove of trees was your cathedral
and God spoke to you
on the wind that stirs the grass.

I will look for you
in the still place between each breath
and know you are with me.

Hearts and shadows

climb into early light
head for the summit
as you strain upwards
the warming sun dips
below crest of hill
plunge into cliff shadow
struggle up to emerge
pant into light again
heart thumps with exertion
the climb hard but worth it
as I surely know you are
my thoughts shout for you
dream you up
where you belong
see how my heart beats
for you for you
my single shadow
sun stretched longs
to tangle with yours
blend into single being
come with me
climb to the sun
merge shadows
and hearts
be one

Other side

the ferry crosses chocolate rippled water
with its cargo of poets
the collective noun for poets in a boat
is a chattersplash

the cathedral is obscured by leaves
the stone is different colours
if I was an artist my palette would be
cream pink terracotta green

sun is bright after indoor coolness
follow the path of orange tip butterfly
smell hawthorn blossom
taste the names of hedgerow plants
comfrey cow parsley archangel

I am watched from the river
by two bulging eyes
which are really the wheels
of a shopping trolley
is this an improvement
on its previous existence?

two swans fly past
necks outstretched wings creaking
low over the water

I am aware of tranquillity
edged with city noise
punctuated by cathedral bells

From the other side

water laps the twelfth step
the ferry can ply its trade today
we climb down into the boat
launch into a rising flood
the river full but still gentle
the boat glides through the water
edges into the stream
the rower pulls long and hard
heads across the current
struggles against the flow
the oars dig deep
brown water swirls
eddies after each stroke
we reach the other bank safely
water trickles from the shipped oars
pools on the muddy floorboards
we climb the steps on the other side
a passenger voices concern
the ferryman slowly replies
we've plied this crossing
for six hundred and fifty years
never lost anyone yet
always eventually found

Beach Walk in Rain

"We could get as far as the Hayle Estuary,"
you said. We felt the first drops of rain
as we crossed Porthmeor Beach
but you said it was just a passing shower.

Near the harbour we smelled frying bacon
climbed down slippery steps onto sand
where gulls' footprints made random patterns.
The rain came down harder.

At the next beach I suggested we turn back.
I was worried because you had no waterproof,
but you were convinced the rain would stop
so we followed the wide sweep of Carbis Bay.

We crossed a wooden railway bridge,
and saw a café glowing with amber light.
There was frothy coffee in paper cups that said
'drinks maybe hot' instead of 'drinks may be hot'.

We watched the gulls grouped on the sand.
"It's your deserted beach," you said with a grin
and I remembered a poem I wrote years before
about running naked in a storm.

Luckily before your imagination ran riot
a group of ramblers stepped onto the sand –
stick figures with umbrellas here and gone.

"Whose idea was this walk?" you asked
as we headed towards the railway station
and sat in the blue painted shelter
sharing chocolate kisses in the rain.

Portheras

I had wandered off the track
where it crossed the cove
via a stone bridge
followed the stream
down to the beach
marvelled at the
wave cut contours

Down the cliff path
in the fading light
he with loaded pack
and long stride reaching
for today's destination
you trailing in his wake
tired legs reddened with effort

'Hello' brought no response
from him from you
a flicker of a smile
wouldn't you rather stop
see how this stream
has carved the
coloured beds of sand

Sit and listen
to the waves
watch the sun
slowly sink down
and set over the bay
But you trudged on
following

Holy Well – Madron

You notice the lichened trees first
then enter into the hushed silence
of the sun dappled glades.

Life still flourishes here
in the curling bracken fronds
and the thick twine of ivy stems.
Pick blackberries, hawthorn, sloes
and taste their magic
feel it draw you in to something deeper.

At the edges of your vision
see the soft footsteps of a young girl
just out of reach in time and space.

Small birds whisper
the ancient secrets of this place.
Cross the wide stone stiles
and enter the remains of the chapel
where flowers are placed on the stone altar.

The girl watches as you make your offering
then follows you back to the well
where the trees bear a strange harvest
of coloured ribbons, scraps of cloth
and old socks.

I write my wish on white paper and tie it to
a lichened branch with red ribbon.
Will the girl read it after I've gone?
Is she part of my healing process
or one of the many selves
who walk with me wherever I go?

Saint Juliot's

would that I should
visit you more often
through the woods
with tumbling stream
legs dragging
across the fields
to rest in silence
here within the
deepness of calm
lit by slant windows
the coolness of peace
from long labour
it will be long
before I come again
many years may pass
but I will think about
your peace and hope
to find it again

18 Folgate Street

It is four o'clock on a winter's afternoon.
The door is liquorice black,
decorated with a holly wreath.
You ring the bell and wait for admittance.
You step into a candlelit hallway.

There are no tour guides, no guide books.
Signs say: 'You either see it or you don't'.
You make your way in silence. Be careful.
The stairs are steep and the ceilings low.

Dark clad figures move in shadowy corners
here and gone like ghosts.

Down in the kitchen there is warmth
and the smell of baking.
Jam tarts on a plate. A ginger cat
watches the canary in its cage.
You hear hoof-beats,
the sound of carriage wheels.

Upstairs, you hear voices in the dining room,
The sound of a fight and a chair overturned.
The smell of roasting meat lingers
a half-eaten apple lies abandoned.

In the next room you see
the remains of afternoon tea in
yellow porcelain cups. Rose perfume lingers.

There is no gift shop as you leave.
Your memories will be enough.

18 Folgate Street

the hushed quiet of the house of the weaver
drifts in time along Folçate street
deep in the heart of Sp ttalfields

harbours the fugitives fled from France
their silk webs interwoven
span the years from cellar to roof

a drama in still life the fitting of objects
their collective presence
signpost the spirit of those times

contours of the past
mood spells of an age
bathed in English light

step through the frame
close your eyes so you can see
enter before it fades

into the room take three steps back,
feel the shape of the house's spirit
looking inside out

apply your hands to the door
crack open at the centre
gently very gently push back both sides

to find the space between

Whitstable

A woman is sweeping out her beach hut
with a birch broom.
I sneak a glance inside,
notice the shelves at the back
lined with books
two wicker chairs and a primus stove
and remember how I envied people
with beach huts
when I was a child.

I think of the pretend tea parties I created
with grey stones for ham sandwiches
brown for honey
and yellow for egg
and how I lined up my dolls
along the breakwater
with mussel shell plates and limpet shell cups.

I remember men with hankies on their heads
knotted at the corners
sitting in deckchairs reading newspapers
and how angrily one reacted
when I accidentally hit him
with a small blue pebble
that escaped from a game of 'five stones.'

Crab and Winkle Way

a westerly greeted us
slapped spray in our faces
from a chopped sea
you remembered the east wind
grey sea and groynes
behind whose black bulk
you huddled for shelter

they finger the sea
stretch away to the distance
fight to stabilize the shingle
a single grain then another
lifted and carried downshore
away to cover the wrecks
on the Goodwin sands

we share the beach with turnstones
oysters and slipper limpets
a brightness of beach huts
one with a lodge of starlings
We found Hog's fennel
on Tankerton's green slopes
and benches in memory of ....

on the point by Long Rock
a newt crossing the path
turned out to be a lizard
then round the curve of beach
to Studd Hill and Hampton
and on to Herne Bay then
coffee and bacon sandwiches on the pier

Treasures

in my memory box
I place a pink slipper limpet
that reminds me of a ballet shoe

a pair of oyster shells
hinged shut like a secret
that may once have contained a pearl

a spiral shell with purple lips
gateway to a magical world
that echoes with the sound of the sea

a piece of blue glass
the colour of the stained glass dragonfly
in my kitchen window

I add an image of fennel and mallow
that grow at the edge of the beach
and pink valerian
the colour of strawberry ice cream
eaten on childhood summer holidays

in my imagination I wade out to sea
and ride one of the white horses
back to shore

Whitstable

would that I could
have stemmed the
smother of London tides
the barrage of filth
that submerged them
the ghosts of English
oysters gape open mouthed
at the invasion of others
foreign friends who cling
and clamp mount anything
solid including themselves
forever trying for size
the slipping down
smooth and silky
till tradition and
industry drowns
as they stick in the throat

Straggle

The other poets thought
the word was negative
but to me it tasted
of evaporated milk
and shortbread biscuits.

As a child I was used to "Hurry up.
Stop scuffing your toes.
Don't straggle."

The taste map of the word
conjures up
feelings of safety
and pictures of gossamer fairies
in the book
Mum read from at bedtime

when I could rest in the velvet tunnel
of my imagination.

Absent

adrift
behind the milling throng
along
the pathway turned aside
explore
the wideness of the day
pause
for distraction to settle

a flick of wing
a petal glance

conscience pricked
there is never time

always
long enough
space
to be caught
somewhere
for a while

liable
to be picked off
at any moment

Iona

someone's left a sandcastle
on the deserted beach
where rain clouds gather
and Staffa's shadow looms
like a surfacing submarine
far out to sea

I see echoes of Fingal's Cave
in the thrift and shell patterned castle

only our footprints
soon to be washed by the tide
disturb the magic

Driven

Scuds of dirty white foam
drive up the beach
angry waves
pebble shift on shore
salt and sand
sting the cheeks
head down into the wind
habit billowing behind
a Nun searches just
above the tides reach
burrows into the wet shingle
with the faith she has
that guides her hands
she knows she
will find and feel
the sea smoothed stone
of St. Columba's marble

Tiddesley Wood

deep in the wood
amid the late December
ash saplings

we found the fairy queen's
Christmas tree forest

to ordinary mortals
it looks like emerald green moss
climbing honeysuckle ropes
but you only have to look beyond
to see the pathways between
and imagine the tumbling lights
of a thousand fairy lanterns

ignore the roar of the wind
in the tops of the trees
and listen to the whisper
of the age old story
being retold in the magic forest's heart

The wood of Tidi

still early yet the sun already beats down
stride out for the old woods shade
glad of the cool along the tall hedge
ravens croak awake the morning
sport above the green canopies

sink into quiet shade as you enter
wooded since the age of ice
Tidi worked here 800 years ago
huge old coppice stools moss coated
multi trunked proclaim it so

the ride a riot of yellow purple cream
evening primrose fleabane scented agrimony
willowherb loosestrife devil's bit scabious
meadowsweet small teasel blackberry blossom
where the white admirables glide down to feed

here a 'Fall' of trees newly coppiced
a fence protects from gnawing teeth of deer
tall oak 'Whitepoles' left to cut 14 years from now
taller oak 'Blackpoles' left to cut a further 14 years on
and so the cycle continues round

Geological laboratory

spouting hot springs
bubbling mud pools
volcanoes under ice
chaos of fire and frost

tectonic plates meet
Europe and North America
bananas grow in greenhouses
on geothermal fields

wild untamed landscape
dwarf birches and flowers
cold grey sea with strong currents
next stop America

black sand
glittering waterfalls
sudden storms here and gone
leave behind rainbows

By the wind sailor

on a monochrome beach
grey waves thump on shore
white foam sucks into black sand
below basalt columns that tower to sky
storm squalls scud in then clear away
each time the sheet is scoured clean
as pale sun lights the salt haze
that hovers above the shore

a silver strand of sand eel
tossed up by a pounding sea
the split spine coinage of fish
bones bleached and spread
a sickly fulmar on the strandline
among gaudy plastic flotsam
the mottled carcass of a seal
oozes away into black sand

sinistral sails at the winds mercy
shipwrecked on an alien shore
stranded flecks of luminous blue
dessicate and die turn to
thin growth ringed scales
polished by the black grains
and still they ride with the wind
that whips along the shore

Mrs Humphrey's House 1835-36

She was mother to thirteen children,
midwife, nurse to the sick,
layer out of the dead.

She leased the stone house
near Stromness harbour
nursed twenty six whale men
frozen in Arctic sea-ice
frost-bitten, scurvy-ridden, near death.

Oil from whale blubber fuelled lights,
baleen from the mouth made coach springs,
ribs for corsets and umbrellas.

Symptoms of scurvy develop fast
fatigue, bleeding gums, joint pain,
wounds that don't heal, shortness of breath
death from heart failure.

Mrs Humphreys nursed them
but was she Florence Nightingale
or gin-soaked Sairey Gamp?
No one knows.

The Selkie's song

follow the burn the foaming burn
where the brown water twists and boils
set out on the flowing journey
round and round in circles and coils
sail on down to the sea and the shore
come down come down and visit me
I'll carve you a sweet sounding whistle
from the hollow wing of a bird
to play the liveliest lilting air
made from kittiwake or fulmar bone
hear the clear notes above the sea's roar
come down come down and play with me

I'll stitch you the finest of slippers
from the whitest of cuttle bones
so you can dance down by the moonlit sea
and whirl away the hours of night
until the bright dawn light does break
come down come down and dance with me
I'll build you a lovely little house
from drifted wood the tide has brought
with warm floors of sand to step upon
and line the bed with soft eider down
so you can lay down your weary head and sleep
come down come down and dream with me

dream of sweet journeys long and deep
lulled by the softly lapping waves
away away and down and down
 far out under the restless sea
to where the otters seals and fishes sleep
come down come down and drown with me

Meditation

knock and the door will be opened
face your fear
and the light will overcome it
your demons are not real
however powerful they seem

we are all connected
what you do to me
you do to everyone on earth
for we are all part of the web of life

don't be afraid to step away
from your comfort zones
it is only by leaving one shore
that you can discover another

leap and the net will appear
what you know is not all there is
you can only go so far with the light
be prepared to face uncertainty

let go of what is in your hand
before you can embrace the new

Farewell

I have followed in the footsteps of the tow,
sheltered beneath arched bridges and watched
soft rain dimple, winds wave, and storm chop to foam,
the slow silent flow that funnels to your locks.

Fed bold mallard and shy nodding moorhen,
the stately swans that ply your reed fringed ways.
Shared warmth and light with flowers,
butterfly, dragon, and damsel bright.

Watched the solemnity of summer barges,
laden with holidaymakers in search of peace,
stir the mud of centuries once more, that
settles and clears as the season fades.

Feasted on berries black and acid tang of sloe.
Watched as cut reeds, fallen leaves, pile your gates.
Each time they creak open a new display,
patterning the water, that changes every day.

Damp drip of swirling mist as fieldfare and redwing
harvest hip and haw, strip the berried trees bare.
I have watched you turn through another year
knowing I too must tread a path into the new.

May Hill

We have come to pay homage to you
on your special day.
Many times we have seen you
from the motorway
added you to our list of places to visit.

As we enter the grove of pines on your summit
we notice a drop in temperature
as if the spirits of this place have gathered
for their own celebration.

We walk around outside of the circle of trees
notice ponies grazing
their rough coats a range of colours
from cream to caramel, chocolate and black.

A black and white foal follows its mother on shaky legs.
They ignore us as we walk past,
boots sinking into soft grass.
Overhead a buzzard mews as he patrols the thermals
between England and Wales, earth and heaven.

Sometime after 5.17am

we climb to greet month and day
follow their passage through the dew
soles imprinted in soft earth
in the wood crushed bells of blue
the garlic tang of Ramsons underfoot
they loom out of the semi darkness
startle the horses that roam the hilltop
gather and shiver in predawn coolness
huddle together under the old pines
the heat from their bodies rising

the golden orb breaks over Cotswold
reaches slowly across the vale
lights the glistening S of Severn
adds long shadows to the trees
stretches over and enters Wales
choose the tune to greet the dawn
and prance the merry month away
search north to Malvern beacon
cross the Vale for Panorama tower
where others dance to celebrate

trace the patterns weaved
worn in grass by stepping feet
pieces of bark ripped from sticks
a strip of colour loosed from a coat
by the energy of the dance
to crown it all stop and listen
to the first clear Cuckoo's call
the elongated 'oooooo'
lifts from the woods below
echoes in the still spring air

Royal Mail

Our boatman wore a pale blue shirt
with a red Royal Mail logo.
"My Dad's," he said. "He gets paid
ten pounds a week
to deliver the mail to Bardsey.
He doesn't like the shirts though
and they never wear out." He pauses.
"The only thing I don't like is the logo.
I don't know what they put it on with.
I've tried to unpick it and you can't."

"There's no coffee at the farm today.
They're visiting friends in the Outer Hebrides."

We take the dusty track towards farm and abbey.
A woman unlocks a low white building
and we buy cans of ginger beer and yogurt bars.

Murky light filters through the dusty windows
as we look at wicker baskets, felted bags,
natural cosmetics and enamel jewellery.
I buy a small blue boat pendant
to remind me of our journey here
the colour of the sea and sky
and inspire more creative journeys.
There is no till – just an honesty box.

We sit outside to eat our yogurt bars
accompanied by two goats, a young turkey
and a black and white farm dog.
There is no traffic noise
just the piping call of oyster catchers
and the mournful song of the seals.

Island of the Bards

vIsit the ruins of St. Mary's church where the
holy well in the cave below gives fresh water at low tide
here the pilgrims gathered stared out over the sound
the humped whale lit by sunbeams through dark clouds
three trips to the island equalled one to Rome

see the red beaked and legged choughs
hang in the wind at the cliff's edge
journey round to the launching point
climb aboard the twin hulls clamped to the trailer
the tractor pushes it down the steep ramp to sea

twin engines roar into life churn water to foam
the boat surges forward on the island journey
On high buzzard and peregrine quarter the cliffs
below clownish puffins spitting fulmars black guillemots
chocolate razorbills with white eye stripes

Manx shearwaters safe in their burrows wait for night
In the bay grey Atlantic seals lie out on the rocks
sing their mournful songs to the sea
oyster catchers pipe us ashore
the fields are alive with tortoiseshell skipper and blue

together with six spot burnet moths
all have made the journey just like us
drink in the wide open space
quietness peace and calm
the pilgrimage now complete

The fairy glen

the trees of faery are all here
oak ash and thorn
set amongst ferns and green moss
where peat brown water
foams white over rocks

walk carefully down the steep slate steps
surrounded by birdsong
until you reach the bottom of the gorge
look up through a patchwork of green
to where the sun spills through a gap in the clouds

smell the incense left burning by the last visitors
watch the spiral of speckled woods into blue sky
sit and wait for the fairies to come
leave an offering by the mossy roots of an oak
carry their peaceful spirit in your heart always

Fairy glen

approach along the track that winds
through the trees high above the river
shadow and sunlight dapples yellow
cow wheat that overhangs the path

descend the rough cut steps worn by
countless feet down into the shaded gorge
trees overhang the rock strewn river bed
clamber from boulder to boulder

across tree trunks jammed between
pocketed hollows waterworn fairy purses
hold rounded pennies that wait
to be spent with the next flood

black peat mirrors reflect green
leaf and branch blue sky white cloud
others opaqued in cream foam circle
around then lift and drift on the breeze

on the far side a small cave with rock
wallpaper black and white striped
sit and soak up the magic atmosphere
then leave a small token of thanks

Journey

a new road
stretches in front of us
a straight line between wheat prairies
dark brown earth
just showing green

further on a cloud of seagulls
follows a red tractor
below moody grey sky
power lines march across the flat landscape
like rows of paper dolls or an army of aliens

Journey

sometimes they let me out into the forest
to collect the fallen branches
found the gypsies camped in a glade
free to roam they would help me
for a price but when next I sought
that path again the glade was bare

I carried the wood back to High Beach
incarcerated in the asylum there
I could not stand the confinement
like the enclosures ringing round my head
Cowper Green Langley Bush Swordy Well
I must see Mary again - go soon - go Now

the long road stretches to the orison's edge
my boots are worn feet blistered bleeding
no food just grass upon the verge
lay my head to the pole star under the hedge
wake wet with dew stumble on till I see
once more the spire to heaven's glint

the blur of miles and days over now
Helpston - my Mary - home

Evesham - riverbank

This morning the fields are white.
An eerie mist rises from the river
and I watch nervously expecting to see
a hand with a sword rise from the depths
or a witch in a walnut shell boat.

Icy water drips from the trees.
My hands and the tips of my ears
sting with cold.
In the distance I hear a departing train
and the roar of traffic.

Squadrons of Canadas
slice the frozen air
and sink into the misty water.
The glare of the orange sun
outshines the early morning headlights.

Rush Hour

black necks outstretched
five geese slice the centre arch
the leader honks as if to warn
those travelling upstream

they plane down
fan across the river
the green of reflected trees
broken by the cut V's sparkle

the town stirs
traffic clogs the bridge
the longness of narrowboats
lines the quay

from Alvechurch Barbridge
Debdale Wharf and further afield
with names like 'Little Grebe'
and 'Ouzel' and 'Reed warbler'

but best of all is
'Plod'
how lovely it would be
to do just that

Blue Pig Gallery Lewis

I am fascinated by the small net bags
tied with red ribbon
that contain memory fragments -
sea glass, pottery, shells, wood
found on local beaches

things that prompt a sense of place
physical, cultural and spiritual

they call it 'dualchas' in Gaelic

a stirring of memory
the echoes of past lives
that become part of the present

the narrative hidden in an object –
a button, a scrap of fabric or a lost earring –

that becomes a new chapter
in a never-ending story

Time and Tide

the bell stands on a deserted shore
a pebbles throw from the graveyard
that looks out over the bay
may my last resting place be
by the sound of the surge of the sea

the bell stands between land and sea
a time piece and a time marker
speaking in celebration
speaking in loss
a mouthpiece for our culture

the bell stands greened by the sea
sings of swells beneath the stars
rings for all those who
set sail in sorrow or in joy
tolls for those who sleep below

the bell stands at the Atlantic's edge
waves without change without pity
break on the shell sand of the beach
the bell peals with every tide
rung by the ceaseless surge of the sea

Callanish

The evening air smells of heather and salt
as we walk the deserted lanes
past derelict crofts.

The stones stand like silent figures
surrounded by the clamour of voices and wild action
of those who do not feel their magic.

There is a timelessness here
and a sense of peace
that has been missing from my life of late.

I touch the central stone
feel its warmth resonate like a heartbeat
as I make my wishes for a peaceful,
happy and successful life.

The setting sun gilds the sky
behind the distant hills
and I hear the bubbling cry of a curlew.

Calanais

the tall stones stand proud against
cloud capped mountain and mirrored loch
sleeping beauty drowses on the skyline
the bubble of curlew honk of geese
and eerie feathered drum of snipe
is magnified by the dusk quietness
pale lichen beards the edge
of each craggy individual
tonight we are alone with them
finally come to pay our respects
it has been a long time building
but nothing compared to their standing
the pull has strengthened for many years
until it could not be resisted anymore
a faint buzz sounds around the stones
a background hiss in the air
like static from electricity pylons
In amongst them now feel their warmth
vibrations from deep within the earth
pulse upwards to the surface
recharge our spent batteries

Tyn y Cwm

Artists Valley
the neglected garden
that once hummed with life and tea trays

pink camellia blossoms
falling
no chaffinches
no tables
no cream teas

only the sound of the wind in the trees
and the endless babble of the shallow stream

a shaft of sunlight
illuminates the single track
through the fairytale forest
the mossy bridge a gateway to the world beyond

as we turn back down the hill
I notice the remains of a gatepost
that momentarily looks like
a hooded figure standing in the shadows

Estuary

mouth open wide to accept the inevitable
that slides with an almost imperceptible rustle
bubbles and froths at the edges

licks the mud banks clean as she comes
rain patterns the surface sheen
as it quickens to a swirling stream

Greenshank pace and probe the rising tide
a flash of blue and whistle of Kingfisher
as they skim over from the far bank

Mergansers dive then resurface
cut v's as they swim against the flow
Lapwing sport above the fringing marsh

a solitary Curlew patrols the other side
and the sentinel Herons stand guard
as the water gradually deepens.

on a rusted oil drum midstream
a Cormorant preens its wings
readies itself for the first dive

Dream

a sinister circle of black Bath chairs
waits for a lakeside steamer

there are muffled announcements
over an unseen tannoy

the wooden jetty has glass windows
so none can escape

the women in charge wear Victorian dresses
in black bombazine

the giant clock hanging below dark clouds says 3.30
 puffs of smoke appear in the distance

the alarm clock shrills white light

Miner

Honeysuckle twines up sapling Birch
strangles tight against silver bark
a tiny track to start explores twists
before it turns back into itself
then strikes out into a wider path
heads first here and then there
now broad a pale road that leads
to nowhere a whole life travelling
a solitary way wandering through
the greenness of a single leaf

Before the workshop – Chawton

I pause on my way to Jane's house
under grey skies with patches of blue
surrounded by the clamour of birdsong
and the insistent chirp of a sparrow.

I hear the faint roar of traffic on the A31
notice lights on in Cassandra's Cup Café
have a feeling of going back in time as
I look through the windows of Jane's house

see forget me nots in a vase
a quill pen on a bureau
a shadow in a corner
here and gone.

Selborne

follow the zigzag path up the hanger
adorned by wood anemones
onto the old common where
wind blown beech and oak spreadeagle
over a dogs mercury carpet
turn down the sunken green lane
overhung with blackthorn blossom
out into the sun across open fields

skylarks serenade over spears of wheat
as you follow along the hedge
with violets purpling the banks
and wild garlic in the wet bottoms
on to the coppice where the
bright green of wood spurge
and lemon yellow of primrose
with bluebells nearly flowering

cowslips line the track where
long ropes of old man's beard
dangle down into the pathway
woodpeckers drum overhead
back into the hanger and on a
rotting fallen tree the delicate
white flowers of wood sorrel
nod in the cool breeze

finally reach the Wakes where
marsh marigolds glow in the pond
with fritillaries in the wild garden
their chequered bells beaded with
water droplets after the shower

Cragg Sisters Tea Room – Aldeburgh

"Studying tea is not unlike studying wine,"
she says in her smoky voice
as she recommends the Star of India tea.

I gaze around at the posters from
1940s 'Picturegoer' magazines.
'Three Coins in a Fountain' plays in the background.

The tables are covered with floral plastic cloths.
Each one has a bone china cup and saucer
filled with anemones
and exotic blue birds with silver tails.

There are cake stands, beaded doilies,
tea strainers and sugar tongs.
The time-whirling mis-match of china
revives memories
of those I love but see no longer.

Flint strand

pebbles on the beach rattle your name
slowly being unmade by the sea
clay rinsed away into milky oblivion
millennia hence it will be remade
the sequel once more repeated
into flint nodules on the strand
the names echo yours and the gallery
where you stare over those
same pebbles out to sea
past the steel glint of scallop that
blinds the eye as it rears from shore
your lines a sketch an etch
that seems simple at first
until you sink deeper into
the swell of the waves
the scream of the gulls
the freedom of the wind
scratched in spider spartan lines
cutting through blue

The Boat House

When I first saw you in 1974
your paint was peeling
you looked unloved
a place where nobody came.

I was three days married
aware I'd made the worst mistake
of my life so far.
Seeing you for the first time
still shines as a special memory
in the darkness that surrounded me.

My new husband stood impatiently
while I stood in a daydream
replaying images of Under Milk Wood
inside my head
as I looked at the grey fishing boat bobbing sea
and imagined a sloe black,
slow, black night without fear.

Later, at Brown's Hotel I spoke to two old men
in tweed caps, asked if they'd ever met Dylan
and said how I loved his work.
"He liked a drink," was all they'd say,
winking at each other,
followed by a cagey
"You're not from the press are you?"

Now forty years later, my writing dreams fulfilled
I return, hand in hand with someone special.
You are transformed. I smell coffee,
hear the chatter of visitors.
The sun paints a golden pathway on the sea.

The Worm

Easter, low tides, to get further down
the beach, study the life of the littoral zone.
To dig sea potatoes, heart urchins, catch
edible, spider and velvet swimming crabs.
The hotel on the headland, woken
the first morning by the bleat of sheep
sheltered behind the low wall
from the blizzard of snow.

Crabs and mussels cooked in cider
over a driftwood fire, washed down
with more cider, couples drift away
into darkness under towering cliff.
Later, a summer sunbathing, swimming,
trudging up and down the beach path.
Rock pooling, building sand castles
the incoming tide always washes away.

Now, step on stones across a river,
drown in wild garlic deep in the woods.
Watch the tragic comedy of a duck
that tried, but failed, to eat a frog.
Found those same fragile hearts
as far apart as Ynyslas and Luskentyre
wrapped and carried them reverentially
home and added to the collection.

Hang gliders cruise edge of cliff in front
of setting sun, disappear behind the wall
that the sheep sheltered behind. We dine
in a restaurant that was once a laboratory.

About the Authors

Sue Johnson is a poet, short story writer & novelist. Her other interests include reading, walking & yoga.

Sue is a Writing Magazine Creative Writing Tutor & also runs her own brand of writing workshops.

Born & bred & still living in the Vale of Evesham Bob Woodroofe's poems appear in many poetry magazines & are performed locally.

Inspired by the natural world, the landscape & local tradition he attempts to bring the magic of nature & its restorative & healing qualities to a wider audience.

Also available from the

Greenwood Press
38 Birch Avenue
Evesham
Worcs. WR11 1YJ

website http://greenwoodpress.co.uk

e-mail info@greenwoodpress.co.uk

by Bob Woodroofe

A trilogy of poetry collections from
life & nature in the Vale of Evesham

Nature, Reflections & Spirit of the Vale

In search of greenness

Something Stirred

the Poetry Collection

Pick of the crop

Joint poetry collections by
Sue Johnson & Bob Woodroofe

Tales of Trees & Journey

Creative Writing books
by Sue Johnson

Writer's Toolkit & Writer's Toolkit 2, 3 & 4

www.ingramcontent.com/pod-product-compliance
Lightning Source LLC
Chambersburg PA
CBHW061343040426

42444CB00011B/3060